of Marriage

♀ Marriage

NICOLE COOLEY

Alice James Books
Farmington, Maine
www.alicejamesbooks.org

10 9 8 7 6 5 4 3 2 1

Alice James Books are published by Alice James Poetry Cooperative, Inc., an affiliate of the University of Maine at Farmington.

Alice James Books
114 Prescott Street
Farmington, ME 04938
www.alicejamesbooks.org

Names: Cooley, Nicole, author.
Title: Of marriage / Nicole Cooley.
Description: Farmington, ME : Alice James Books, [2018]
Identifiers: LCCN 2017052421 | ISBN 9781938584770 (softcover : acid-free
    paper)
Classification: LCC PS3553.O5647 A6 2018 | DDC 811/.54--dc23
LC record available at https://lccn.loc.gov/2017052421

Alice James Books gratefully acknowledges support from individual donors, private foundations, the University of Maine at Farmington, the National Endowment for the Arts, and the Amazon Literary Partnership.

Cover painting: "Reflection" by Samantha French

Contents

For Ruth and Paul Cooley, m. 1929-2000
and for Jacki and Peter Cooley, m. 1965-2018

4

"What is marriage, is marriage protection or religion, is marriage renunciation or abundance, is marriage a stepping-stone or an end. what is marriage."

—Gertrude Stein, *Operas and Plays*

Marriage in Mixed Media, Acrylic, Canvas, Pixels

In a tapas bar I'm alone eating food you hate—cracker stained with black squid,
spoonful of sea urchin, this tiny plate of eggs and olives.

I love food that is all sharp edges, brackish and salt, iced mineral
water that burns the tongue and hisses in its glass bottle

like the silver grape our daughter stole at a liquor store fruit display,
so transparent it was irresistible, miniature crystal cracking

in her palm. Now I tip a teaspoon of salt
onto my plate. Remembering how after

you left I slipped my hands in the pocket of your jacket,
then bent closer, tongued its empty cool silk.

Do you think I'm talking about your body?
Do you think I'm talking about sex, my fork splitting metal on a plate,

you eating too fast with your fingers?
Do you think I'm talking about marriage or

our bedroom, windows rain-flushed and dark, or
our meeting here, now, naked on the kitchen's cold linoleum?

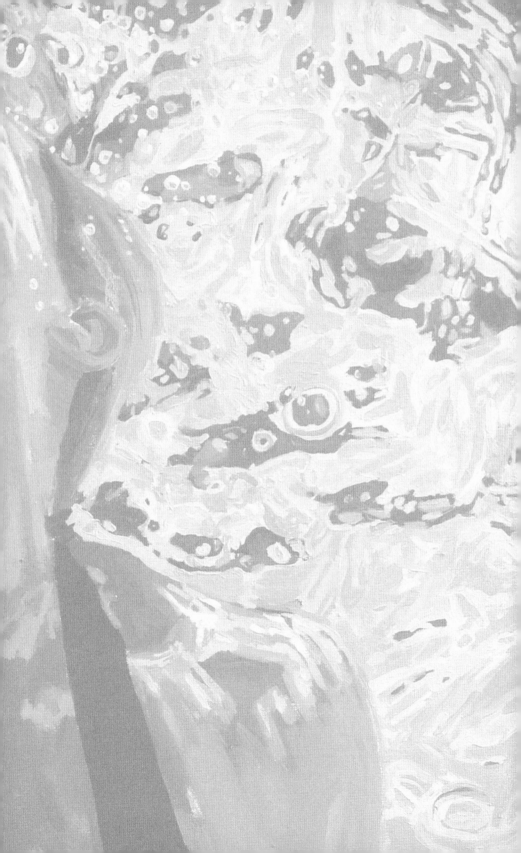

Marriage Tanka

i.

When Shakespeare's Coriolanus greeted his wife, he called her "my gracious silence." Or was it not "my greatest silence?"

ii.

Build a Shrine to the Unlucky. To the Misfortunate. The Tubercular Wife who died too early, lungs wool-clotted.

iii.

The wild roses climb the fence like bad girls, into the neighbor's yard, ravenous, then as we sleep at night—gasoline drowned.

iv.

Outside, the street furred with dark. In our bedroom, my legs hooked over your shoulders. Cold lamplight erases the night sky clean.

v.

In Spenser's *Amoretti* the beloved never speaks back. I swallow the poems like bad candy, choke on the wife.

vi.

Marriage: over and over a retelling. A dress to wear for days on end. A dress to shuck off, stuff under the bed.

vii.

Husbandless: a bowl of dry ice. Husbandless: thimble to protect a finger, little silver stump. Husbanded.

viii.

The *cassone,* or marriage chest, given to the bride by her parents at the wedding. Gold, to hold her clothes. Most resembles a casket.

ix.

Green lush silence is its own shrine to marriage. As is the wife who did not die. The wife who wore the tight black wedding dress.

Erasing *Marriage: Its Origin, Uses, and Duties, 1850*

some resemblance   in the union of heat and light

in the sun   its winterly inanimate state

two who are united said to be no more twain but one flesh

wrought out in   neglect   or violation

frequently more ardent   as in its singleness

conjugal love   like the bud   flower as yet folded and wrapped

marriage unfolds and makes it sensible

odors of its delicate   exhaled   distilled

state of wedlock   dust of the ground   peculiar to the body

or perhaps love is merely—

Marriage, *noun*

Affinity; alienation; alliance.

Betroth, please be my better half, bigamy, breach of promise.

Couple; confederation; contract.

Divorce by phone service; dowry.

Extramarital; espousal.

Forced marriage. Finished. Final.

Given to this man. Guilt. Gift-wrapped pink package. Gilded Lily.

Had others before, must pretend there were no others.

I extinguished. Later by children.

Jurisdiction: marriage law by law, state by state.

Kinship, in anthropological circles.

Locked in, locked out; hands locked together in sleep.

Married person, mate; match; matrimony.

Nuptials.

Oneness, unity.

Pledge your troth; polygamy.

Quiet now, someone is listening. Someone is speaking vows.

Run. Ran. I ran past him,

Schism; spouse; sacrament.

Trial marriage; tie that binds.

Unity. Untidy.

Vow, violation.

Wedding; who said you are such a willful girl?

X marks the place where we stood at the altar.

You, my beloved, my only. Others will pretend not.

Signed, a marriage decree, an unsteady X, by—

Marriage, a Zuihitsu

When we fight, I make and unmake our bed, fold the sheets with small blue flowers in the shapes of stars to imitate the sky, unmake a space for us to slide inside.

But instead we're back together in a subway tunnel slicked with dark, in a train's sway and swerve, bodies against bodies—above us, sky dense with late summer light, sky 9/11 blue.

Or we're in the car, we're on the coast, we're—in the language of our grandparents—taking a drive through my childhood, our imagined Packard, picnic basket packed, bag of chipped ice in the trunk.

Subway clumsy in a tunnel.

Mississippi empty lot a string across a driveway. Empty lot: slanted pipes for gas lines stuck in the sand. Cicadas hissing in the trees, invisible, dirt below green needles and pine cones.

Pink ice fills our cups.

Through Mobile, Gulfport, Biloxi, Pass Christian. The girls lulled with heat and sleep. Past raised houses, past hibiscus, past Live Croakers, past the Bird Sanctuary, past the Army Corps of Engineers Housing. Sand the color of milk.

Train a tongue in a mouth.

Bodies against bodies.

Under our bed is another world, branched and tunneled, where we could hide, where we could twine our bodies, knit our bones together, in the shimmer of river water, in the quiet magic space of marriage no one sees.

When we fight—

Under our bed is a river, lit and glittering.

Or the girls are double-Dutching on Dauphin Island with a borrowed rope, beside the signs *For Sale Beach Access*, *Do Not Demo*, and *Sea Level Construction* while I imagine you run water for our bath, shove the brush through my hair, scrape it down my back.

Sway and swerve of bodies tossed together in a train.

Small blue flowers in the shape of stars.

Making and unmaking.

Train a tongue in a mouth. Girls lulled with heat and sleep.

You run water for our bath.

We turn toward each other in the night. River always warm and rushing.
Never a skin of ice.

a vinculo matrimonii

Latin, from the bond of marriage

Crinkle and pitch of the bed—we're wrapped in the wedding sheets,

we're spreading a towel on the sand, we're in a backyard hammock,

rain running through it. We're roped.

We're stitched

with loose, looped yarn. We're threaded. We're the quilt still

unfinished, unbacked, unraveling, batting loosened.

We're the blue and white receiving blankets

wrapping the girls' infant bodies.

We're tiny flannel squares of lost.

Blindfold me with

a bolt of cloth unfolding.

Strip the sheets off the bed and let's ladder out of here together—

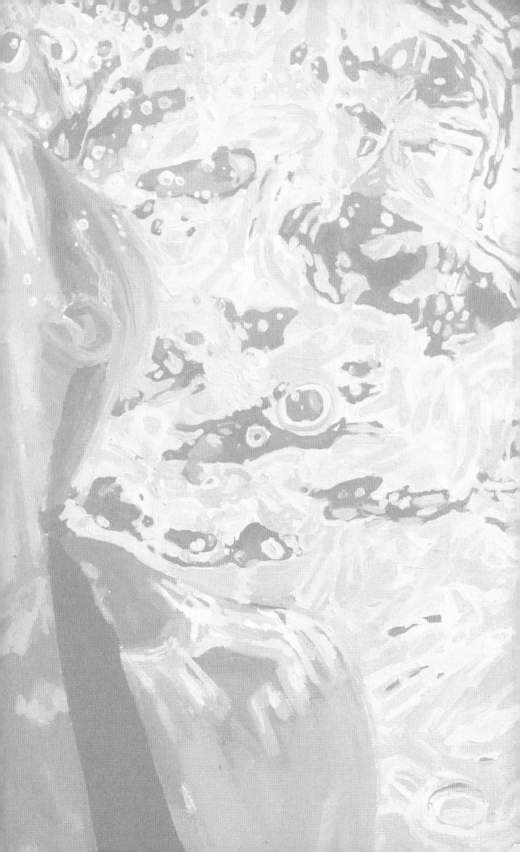

Marriage as a Skateboard Flung off a Bridge

and into a creek, graffitied, stickered red,
wheels chipping and sticking on asphalt, on grass.

You want the skate park's
clean lines, its lovely concave shape,
its bowl reflecting light, but, this, instead:

you're mud-stuck, in a bog, your knees scattered with gravel
you want to lick off, swallow down, but you know

you'd choke.

Marriage as Rock Quarry

We're phosphorus, we're this glowing
rock under UV light in the mineral shed.

We're violet, saffron, we're bright
green. Love, we're all secret silver flicker.

Marriage as Light Socket

Loss: as if you could lock your teeth against it.
Or slam the front door to keep it out.

To keep the baby safe, we sealed the house
as if against bad weather.
Nailed our dresser to the wall,
plugged the outlets up with plastic
to shut them up.

Marriage as Koi Pond

Scrape the pot into the sink, another burned surface,
then another brick-red linen cloth to sheet the table.
Follow me to the yard where the fish
drift like cool dimes on the water, where
I drop my dress, a slur of mesh and lace.

Marriage as Construction Paper

You shut inside yourself, again.
In the bedsheets white as aspirin, with the paper
Fortune-teller folded into triangles
to tell its secrets. Yes. No. Maybe.
You took yourself from me again.

Marriage as a Roll of Aluminum Foil

Wife of cardboard. Husband of twine.
In the kitchen, avocados soften, blacken in the wedding bowl.
The sun: a bitter yellow lozenge.

Marriage as a Velvet-Lined Saxophone Case

Plush and restless, rotted,
this body wants to fold inside
your own. Remember

how we knelt at that altar,
the soles of my wedding shoes flashing back
like red tongues.

Marriage as Chinese Jump Rope

Red and black twined rubber band binding
two girls on the playground together—
turn and flip and twist.
Pull the elastic around my ankles tight.
You don't know what I'm talking about, do you?

Marriage as Motel 6 on Airline Highway

Tonight I rinse my black tights in the sink, twist the nylon tight.

Across the room you sleep without me.
What to do with my empty side.

Black it with rot, black it with burning.

Marriage as the Breakfast Menu at La Habana

Divorced Eggs: one with red sauce, one with salsa verde.
Beside each other, side by side, like breasts on a plate.

Marriage as the C Train to Brooklyn

Beside me the man bites the hospital bracelet off the woman's wrist,

tears white plastic tape with his teeth.

Marriage as Blood Draw

Bruise me, slip the needle badly
into my arm. Scrape me with the heavy metal door
as you slam out. I don't want
to cross the street alone,
not in the light, not in the dark.

Marriage as a Vine That Climbs the Porch

and forces the siding off the house like loose skin

and we want to chop it down but can't

and it's weed fused into wood, weed that wrecks

and saves the house.

Marriage as a Salad Fork

Don't set it on the plate's wrong side, on
the napkin's incorrect edge.

Arrangement is all. The plate is cold in your hands.

Remember the stutter of blue flowers
I gave you, in a plastic cup?

Marriage as a Plate of Spinach

Leaves bottle-green as a dress, the wrong dress,
the one you took from my closet,
let fall over my shoulders to the floor.
Leave it there.
In my favorite fairy tale, all the bad mother desires
is sharp-leaved rampion.
She gives up her first child.
I said, drop the dress right now.
Come here.

Marriage as Thrift Shop Coat

with a fur collar that circles like a noose
with sleeves that itch my wrists
with buttons that yank too tight over my breasts.

I step out on the black-and-white tiled floor
and wrap my arms around you. Please don't leave.

From *Marriage, A Dictionary*

On Shock

Sudden blow   bundle of grain   a *surprise*   *a heap of sheaves meaning trade*
with the Dutch

A thick mass of your hair on the brush   in the pillow   in my mouth

When an electric current passes through all or part of the body

How I wish to *collide violently* with myself

To throw troops into confusion by charging at them

The shock of cold water   the shock of wedding cake shoved
in my mouth

Stuttering heartbeat felt by a hand on the chest wall

A knife in a light socket

Pile or stack of unthreshed corn

And what is myself without you

Push your hair into my mouth

Will you *collide violently* with me

Will you be a decision inflicted upon my body

A bundle   unthreshed and untethered

The shock of

Jar   impact   collapse

Flash of my white nightgown in our dark yard

On Displeasure

A groom's cake is most often a fruitcake, molasses-dark,
studded with orange, with green, cake to stick in a wife's throat.

From *Middle French: desplaisir.*

Oh, little bitter one,
let me keep you away from the wedding,
let me hide you under my bed.

You are not the cake we wanted. You are all
.

irritation and *vexation.*

A clot in my mouth. Little *disrelish.*

Archaic: a cause of injury.

You don't drip off a chin, you stutter
on my tongue, oh little antipathy, you don't seduce anyone.

On Secrecy

The color of vinegar poured into a beaker

Not known or seen   not meant to be known or seen by others

A glass bead hidden in the mouth

From Latin: secretus   separate   set apart

Once I told you I wished I was made of rainwater

Revealed only to the initiated

You told me not to speak of it with anyone

The fine flax thread used in orphanages for lace-making

Once I told you

Hole-in-corner   hush-hush   undercover   underhanded

At the edge of the Dutch painting a girl holds a pillow over a pricked pattern
loops thread around a bobbin in a corner of a dark room
A girl no one is watching twines lace out of human hair

On Private

I snap off the bedside lamp, its metal pull-string like a wayward
    tongue.

A soldier of the lowest rank.

Of safekeeping. Of shutting the bedroom door.

Confined to or intended only for the persons immediately concerned.

I unpin my skirt at the waist.

From Middle English: taken away

Tête-à-tête. Sub rosa.

A body scissored on the floor and waiting.

Of safekeeping.

From the Latin for bereave, from the Latin for deprive.

On Apology, on Want

Mortar and pestle grind my spices to ash

But what I want most is a broad chalkboard sweep—

An expression of regret

What I want most is to share a plate of mineral salt-white

An admission of guilt

I want the brackish   the ruined   I want limestone and gravel
in my mouth

From apo—away + logia—

What I want   *reason plea alibi*

Of Marriage, of Glass Gardens

After Dale Chihuly's exhibit, *Garden and Glass*

Inside, sheaf after sheaf, glass
strawed into gold, glass wicked into flame-colored weeds,

blown into seedpod, trumpet flower.

We stand together in the glass garden made of sand and fire.

The desire is to *blow the glass almost to the point of collapse—*

▣

Let's climb inside *Mille Fiori*: Italian for one thousand flowers.
Let's stand among the fragile reeds, glass leaves that you swear shiver
when we pass.

▣

Marriage: a sheet of black plexiglass that acts as a mirror whether you want it or not.

Marriage: a surface on which the installation's cool tubes are grounded, piped,
driven into wood.

Marriage: the process the gaffer describes as *how to stabilize the molecular structure
of the glass—*

Marriage: the glass is luminous but never lit from within. The glass is all refracted light.

Marriage: the artist's desire: *to use all the colors in the hot shop—*

◘

This is *immersive*—this glass, this light, this love?

◘

Imagine a glass flower circling my shoulders.

Your hands wrap mine. Your hands necklace my spine.

◘

Once upon a time, a couple wandered in a glass forest, hand in hand, past tall reeds, clear glass swans with cobalt beaks. The forest's secret: all glass flowers are hollow as pneumatic tubes, dead cylinders.

None of this is fragile.

◘

To use all the colors—

To the point of collapse—

▣

Marriage: a shiver of glass?

▣

Marriage: how many colors in the palette, in this garden.

Let's float out of here in a boat of glass. Let's be all water and light.

Marriage, the Museum of Papermaking

The first room is dark as an aquarium: bark floats
behind glass. The air cool and loose. This is the beginning.

My hands inside your shirt. My hands sliding
over your back. *Inner bark of trees. White birch.*

Papyrus plants grew thick as a man's wrist beside the Nile.
Remembering. In the second room, parchment couples with vellum,

sheepskin with calfskin. Paper made from flesh. My hands inside.
In the third: *wood pulp can be fashioned into a collar, cuspidor, apron, hat.*

Pull the paper shirt off, over your head, seams scratching.
Last glass case: here is a card composed of small dark windows.

Look into the stereoscope to see the future:
the light was cool and loose that day. My hands on your back.

Our old selves still unlocatable, written and crossed out.

Marriage, the Franklin Mineral Museum

You and I start in the underworld, in the zinc mine,
perfect replica, with a linoleum floor and a mannequin holding

a carbide lamp. We start at the mineral dump at the bottom of the hill.
We start with the rocks. Teaspoon by teaspoon, we dig

in the quarry to find the magic rocks—rocks the color of a pink washcloth
to scrub a baby's leg, her back. Rocks the size of a fist.

The gravel pit is splintered light, all ash and bone, and our daughter wants to talk
about "Patriot Day" in school. Now, the kids are allowed

for the first time to tell their stories. Some weren't born. Most were babies.
B's mother would have died that morning but she was home with him because

he was a baby. The place where she works burned down. Rock a dilated eye. Rocks
glowing green as iceberg lettuce. Fever bright.

Rock a split heart, rock all ventricle, rock-hard arterial under
the earth where the E train rushes, the day I waited

at the escalator at the top of the PATH terminal to tell you
about the baby. Teaspoon by teaspoon. Our daughter wants

me to repeat the story of how I held her on my lap,
how we watched TV while the tunnels shut down,

how we sealed the windows with towels and cloth diapers
to keep the smoke out. Now, at the shack on the hill,

we wash rocks in a bucket of mud water.
We bathe them in mineral light so they light up, too fluorescent.

Flinkite for fidelity. Otavite for hold me close. Albite for
just get up off the mattress.

Rocks spilled and spilling. Too bright—

Take me to the local room. The Fluorescent Room. The Fossil Room.
The safe room. The room without history.

Marriage, Beau Rivage Casino, Biloxi, Mississippi

In the infinity pool filled to its green brim, we look out over a wrecked city.

An oblong of light falls over our girls' bodies while they float in silence.
Outside: large vacant blocks of dirt and crabgrass. The pool smells like sour milk.

The summer air like chalk dust on my fingers. I jam the only flowers I find, purple
weeds from the beach, in the younger daughter's milk carton beside the bed.

In the car, the girls keep a mason jar with two fireflies in the back seat, *a boy and a*
girl, and they are married—

and so the four of us settle into a heart-shaped bed. The casino is so gold,
Arcadia says. The lobby all blurred smoke and people with black trash bags.

Tonight, once the girls sleep, I slip my fingers into your mouth, searching for the
burnt taste of the lost, the missing, a way to explain the empty.

Downstairs, the slot machines glow red and silver for no one.
The bugs bang their wings together, frantic, wanting darkness.

I want to lead you outside, to the waterline, the edge of the Gulf.

I want the burnt taste of it, your mouth, insistent.

We open and open the door.

Marriage, the Old Salem Toy Museum

In the museum, the yellow light is a half lemon floating on the surface
of a drink.

Our daughters' hair threaded with rain. Our daughters running past us.

A small train loops, disappears, and the older girl lifts her hand to the
ceiling: *It's winding!*

In my notebook I write*: The rocking horse was a popular nineteenth-
century studio prop when posed with children.*

But this is my copying, not inhabiting language.

The girls want to touch a rubber horse, lung-colored, a blue cow with
red-stitched skin.

How does a toy become a relic? How does a toy become a talisman?

Together, we love these girls fiercely.

This is inhabiting our life together.

The girls' childhoods already shrinking.

Outside the museum my notebook's pages unfasten from the spine—

The wooden ducks swim away, the cloth chickens stand up, fly out, beyond—

The space between us always shrinking—
How not to just transcribe? How not to copy?

What divides the beginning of a family from the after?

All of it a spell against the missing.

Marriage, Objects

My Pillow from High School in New Orleans

Why do you want it, old souvenir,
spiky with feathers?
I imagine our dust dissolving together,
skin mingling without us.

Ring from the Cambodian Night Market

pearl the color of milk
pearl from a missing necklace
tiny diamonds circling silver
retelling of another woman's story

A Fax Machine

silent under our bed
when you were gone it whirred your voice back
when I missed you most I took the pages to bed

Place Setting, Arkansas, with Painted Chickens

Basement box of dishes no one but us wanted.

Each saucer into which your grandmother
smashed her cigarette ash
in her life as a new widow.

Sonogram Image

This first body caught in my body made by our two bodies
body printed on slippery paper   keepsake body
I lose as soon as we get home

A Copy of Roland Barthes, Mythologies

Another gift to you—
Now I'd say:
Let's play *plastic.* Let's play *striptease.* Let's play *toys*
or *wrestling* or *soap powder.*
Let's play *wine and milk.*
Let's throw a *clear light* on each other.

Mini Bean Doll, Arcadia, Florida

Made in Hong Kong, Mini Bean Dolls live in decorated matchboxes, only the top of their baby-sleepered bodies visible. Baby bodies stuffed inside the matchbox, always half-emerged, tucked in tightly. Always baby, never walking, forever looking as if he would like to escape. The mini bean doll I gave you wears a peaked hat like an elf and sleeps happily in his matchbox. He wears a red baby sleeper, but he most resembles a man.

Your Dictionary

In the slur of January light, midwinter, or on the kitchen floor
scoured to raw yet still unswept, you show me

your dictionary app on your phone and I say—

—*take me*—

while outside, the sky soap-white, moon snapped shut

1950's Salad in My Garage Sale Cookbook

Here is a radish slice curled in an ice tray like a fetus.

The thoughtful wife has a simple beverage (cold in summer, hot in winter) ready for her weary husband when he comes home at night.

Here is a shot glass of tomato sauerkraut juice.

I stir each glass with what is called a *muddler:* carrot stick piercing
a pitted olive.

I show you my favorite page: how to set an attractive marriage table: damask
linen, napkins to harmonize.

How to place each water glass directly above the point of each knife.

Of Wedded

Wed, from Old English for *a pledge.*

To be devoted—yes—

yet in my favorite stories why is luck always linked to ruin?

In the Roman Empire, a husband breaks a barley cake over his new bride's head, symbol of fertility.

Remember how I cracked apart frozen pieces of our cake and packed them, brought them to Cambodia to meet you?

Medieval England: spiced buns are piled high and a bride and groom must kiss across the stack without it tumbling to the floor—

I want to be assured—

if the wedded couple does not knock the cake over they are *assured prosperity.*

How to smash and destroy yet still be lucky?

When the cake falls, the wedding guests gather the crumbs into confetti—

once, we slept carefully with pineapple-filled broken slices
under our pillow in a Hong Kong hotel

while moonlight rinsed the bed, while we began our marriage.

Marriage: A Daybook

From the window the river rinses
the dark. I twist
the wedding beads around my neck. I've lost
my ring, silver and antique, bought from the night market
in the other world across
the ocean, color of dull lead,
color of the pan I scrub and burn
in the sink.

◼

Catullus wrote, *I hate and love*, and he wasn't talking about marriage.

◼

Not talking about the blacked-out
window crossed with hurricane tape,
like a movie screen, a page redacted,
your hand erasing a blackboard
with an eraser's soft compliant body.

Acknowledgments

"Marriage, the Museum of Papermaking" and "Marriage, The Old Salem Toy Museum" (as "Incunabula" and "The Speaking Book"), *Blackbird*.

"Marriage, Objects," *The Coachella Review*.

"Marriage in Mixed Media, Acrylic, Canvas, Pixels," (as "Love Poem"), *Columbia Poetry Review*.

"Marriage, the Franklin Mineral Museum," *Connotation Press: An Online Artifact*

"Marriage as a Skateboard Flung off a Bridge," "Marriage as a Vine That Climbs the Porch," and "Marriage as a Salad Fork," *Construction*.

"Marriage, Beau Rivage Casino, Biloxi Mississippi," *The Hampden-Sydney Poetry Review*.

"Marriage Tanka," *North American Review*.

"Marriage as Rock Quarry," Marriage as Light Socket," "Of Marriage, of Glass Gardens," *Narrative*.

"On Secrecy," "On Private" and "On Displeasure," *Plume*.

"Marriage: A Daybook," *Poem-a-Day*, The Academy of American Poets, www.poets.org, January 23, 2014.

"Of Shock," *Poem-a-Day*, The Academy of American Poets, www.poets.org, January 19, 2016.

"Marriage as Construction Paper," "Marriage as a Roll of Aluminum Foil," "Marriage as a Velvet-lined Saxophone Case," "Marriage as Blood Draw," "Marriage as Motel 6 on Airline Highway," "Marriage as Thrift Shop Coat," *Tinker Street.*

"Marriage as Chinese Jump Rope," "Marriage as the Breakfast Menu at La Habana," "Marriage as the C Train to Brooklyn," "Marriage as a Plate of Spinach," were included in *The Plume Anthology of Poetry 2013,* and "Of Wedded" was included in *The Plume Anthology of Poetry 6.*

I am so thankful to Carey Salerno, Julia Bouwsma, and Alyssa Neptune at Alice James Books for their editorial vision and their kindness and generosity. Deep gratitude and love to Pamela Barnett, Alissa Cooley Rowan, Jodi Cressman, Kimiko Hahn, Amelie Hastie, Julia Spicher Kasdorf, Shelley Renee, Talia Schaffer, and all my students at Queens College — The City University of New York. And most of all — my love forever to Alex Hinton.

Book Benefactors

Alice James Books wishes to thank the following individual who generously contributed toward the publication of *Of Marriage*:

Sarah Gordon
Vandana Khanna & Jason George
Mihaela Moscaliuc

For more information about AJB's book benefactor program, contact us via phone or email, or visit alicejamesbooks.org to see a list of forthcoming titles.

Recent Titles from Alice James Books

Alice James Books has been publishing poetry since 1973. The press was founded in Boston, Massachusetts as a cooperative wherein authors performed the day-to-day undertakings of the press. This collaborative element remains viable even today, as authors who publish with the press are also invited to become members of the editorial board and participate in editorial decisions at the press. The editorial board selects manuscripts for publication via the press's annual, national competition, the Alice James Award. AJB remains committed to its founders' original mission to support women poets, while expanding upon the scope to include poets of all genders, backgrounds, and stages of their careers. In keeping with our efforts to foster equity and inclusivity in publishing and the literary arts, AJB seeks out poets whose writing possesses the range, depth, and ability to cultivate empathy in our world and to dynamically push against silence. The press was named for Alice James, sister to William and Henry, whose extraordinary gift for writing went unrecognized during her lifetime.

DESIGNED BY
PAMELA A. CONSOLAZIO

Spark design

Printed by McNaughton & Gunn